For

Overcoming Loss

A Healing Guide

By Rita Freedman, Ph.D.

PETER PAUPER PRESS, INC.
WHITE PLAINS, NEW YORK

*To my patients—who have courageously
faced loss and overcome it.*

Designed by Michel Design

Contents

Introduction

Grief . . . is only the beginning. After a time it becomes something less sharp but larger, too, a more enduring thing called loss.

ANNA QUINDLEN

We live by losing and leaving and letting go. And sooner or later, with more or less pain, we all must come to know that loss is indeed "a lifelong human condition."

JUDITH VIORST

The call came on a rainy Sunday just as I was leaving for the hospital. Though anticipated, it wasn't really expected. That morning I had turned the page on my calendar and counted the days since her surgery, like pearls on the strand she had given me on a recent birthday. My friend's death left me feeling psychologically and spiritually wounded.

We had watched our children grow up together, watched each other grow older, gossiped and giggled and groped our way from one milestone to another. For months I wore those pearls while I suffered the deeply-felt pain of her loss. It seemed that part of my past had died along with my friend.

We are all familiar with loss—for loss is fundamental to life. Built into nature, it confronts us every day. Blossoms fade. One season claims another even as the tide erodes the shore. Loss is part of that ebb and flow, part of the natural cycle of growth and decay.

Though all too common, our losses are uniquely personal. They come in many sizes and shapes.

> *W*hether we've lost
> a job or a home, a
> beloved parent or mate,
> each loss confronts us
> with our helplessness to
> control life. Suddenly
> the world becomes a
> hostile and barren place.

This book is designed to help you

deal with the pain of loss and to overcome it by healing the wounds within. There are no magic formulas or
instant answers here. There is no one
solution to rebuilding life after loss.
There is no right way or wrong way.
There is only *your* way, which you
have to figure out for yourself. You
must learn how to recognize your
loss, to mourn, to cope, to accept,
and eventually to recover. And all this
takes time.

While time often heals, it isn't just the
passage of time that counts. You have
to know what to do with time to help
it heal. Time offers hope and it can be
your best friend if you work with it.
The chapters ahead will show you
how to start moving thoughtfully
through time.

Every loss is a challenge to grow. Yet growth requires change, which is often painful. Deciding to heal doesn't mean giving up your dreams or your memories. It does mean deciding not to give up on yourself and on your future.

Begin somewhere. The first step may be difficult. The destination may be unclear. But that first step will carry you forward on your journey of renewal. This guide can point you in the right direction, but you must find your own way at your own pace. The seasons can't be rushed. Neither can the process of healing your heart.

DEALING WITH DENIAL

Time hangs heavily on the shoulders of sorrow. When loss hits hard, something gets turned off inside. You may feel frozen or numb. There can be a sense of unreality, as if we are merely living in slow motion. Feelings get detoured and often denied.

A year after her father's death, Karen felt chronically depressed but couldn't explain why. She dragged through the day feeling disengaged from life and disconnected from herself. Karen insisted that her marriage was wonderful and her kids were great. "I have everything I ever wanted, so why do I feel so down?"

When her father died, Karen had felt very little grief. Her parents had divorced when she was ten, and soon afterward her Dad moved away. She hadn't been close to him for years. While in therapy, Karen realized that her own daughter was nearly ten, and it now seemed that her father had left them once again. The feelings of abandonment that she had experienced as a child, but never expressed, became clear.

Like Karen, you may be using denial to blunt the impact of a loss. Denial is a handy defense against the pain of reality. It's a pattern of avoidance that acts like an anesthetic to protect you from feelings that threaten to overwhelm. Denial does mask pain, but the wound remains, festering underneath. You can deny loss for months or years and prevent the healing process from taking place. Eventually it will break out, perhaps as insomnia, or fatigue, or chronic low-grade depression, as in Karen's case.

What does denial sound like?

☞ "Don't worry, I'm a survivor so I'll be OK."

☞ "This can't be happening to *me*. It's just not true."

☞ "Oh well, I didn't really want it anyway."

☞ "I can't believe he's gone. I keep thinking he'll walk in any minute."

Have you been using denial as a cover-up? The first step in confronting denial is to stop pretending things are fine when they aren't. You'll need to confront your own false acceptance and face up to your true pain. Symptoms of loss often break through the defense of denial, and may be expressed in your body, in your thoughts, and in your feelings.

Physical symptoms: loss of appetite, binge eating, digestive problems, insomnia, nightmares, fatigue and lethargy, headaches, muscle tension, heart palpitations, hypochondria.

Cognitive symptoms: obsessive thoughts, poor concentration, low motivation, confusion, forgetfulness, slow thinking, perceptual distortions or hallucinations.

Psychological symptoms: emotional swings and loss of control, feeling angry or bitter; nervous,

irritable, restless, tense, or agitated;
anxious, afraid, or helpless; lonely,
guilty or ashamed; sad, weepy, hope-
less, depressed. If you are experiencing some of these symptoms you
should take a hard look at what is
gone and what remains. Face it,
name it, spell it out. Sometimes this
means replacing delicate words like
"passed away" with more truthful
terms: words like "died," "divorced,"
"fired," "rejected," "handicapped,"
"widowed."

Take time to take stock, to count,
recite and recount what has been lost.
You might need to try some confrontations to jolt you out of your
denial: for instance, visiting a grave,
rereading love letters, smelling familiar perfume. Karen pulled out some

childhood photos of herself with her Dad and tried to relive the sorrow she had felt when he left long ago. The pain of his death became clearer as she realized she would never be able to repair that lost bond.

While some losses are obvious and easy to name, others are more subtle, such as lost youth, lost dreams, and lost confidence. These are some of the faces of loss that often get repressed and denied.

*W*hat is now missing from your life as a result of your loss? For healing to begin you must open the protective shell of denial. Recognize, acknowledge, clearly name your losses, and face up to the truth.

TIME OUT FOR ACTIVE GRIEVING

The right to grieve is a precious gift. You don't need anyone else's permission to grieve, but you do need to give it to yourself. Once you stop denying your loss and start recognizing its symptoms, you're ready for active grieving. Because our culture rarely permits the free expression of sorrow, we don't have many good role models to guide us.

Perhaps you equate grieving with self-indulgence or self-pity. Perhaps you're afraid that if you start crying you won't be able to stop and will somehow drown in your tears. And so you withhold permission for the very thing you need most for healing to happen.

Grief is a normal, natural response to any loss. It really is OK not to feel OK. Active grieving has been called the doorway to recovery. You *can* give yourself permission to unlock that door.

What does active grieving look like? You can see, hear, and taste it because it's acted out. When you feel ready and safe, give it a try. Cry out, shout and moan. Pound the table, kick the ground, hit the wall. Wail, weep and whimper. Let your grief run free. These are natural responses to pain and loss, so don't fear them. Tears shed have been called "liquid emotion." Go ahead, taste your rage and drink in your sorrow. Grief that's expressed outward gets released, while grief held inward only keeps on hurting.

Consider when and where you might feel safe enough to act out your feelings. Alone or with a loved one? At home or away? On paper? Active grieving may be spontaneous, but it can also be consciously planned and even rehearsed. In fact, some societies and some religions encourage a prescribed grieving ritual every day for a fixed period of time.

It's important to take some regular time out to find your tears. Drop out of your usual routine and drop into your deeper feelings as you tune in the messages of your mind. You may need to get away completely to focus only on your loss.

People often wonder how long active grieving should continue. That all depends. There is no straight path to overcoming loss. Healing comes in cycles with many ups and downs. Mourning may go on indefinitely after major losses. But active grieving usually diminishes gradually with time, becoming less intense and less overwhelming.

When several family members are suffering from the same loss, they often grieve at very different speeds. We each have personal styles for expressing sorrow, so go at your own pace. Be aware of your changing moods, and just take each day as it comes.

FINDING
SUPPORT

Our lives are built through connections of time and connections with people. Daily events may seem trivial, when seen in isolation. But linked together into weeks and years, they form our cherished history.

The day President John F. Kennedy was killed, millions of phone calls were placed to loved ones, as families united in collective grief. Strangers weeping in the street reached out for one another. I know I'll never forget the image of Jackie and Robert Kennedy holding hands, bonded in sorrow as they walked from the White House.

We are social creatures who crave the comfort of human contact. And we all can use a helping hand on the journey toward healing, especially when the going gets rough. Where can you find the help you need? Don't rely solely on close friends or relatives. There may be comfort when a whole family mourns in a common grief, but there is also loss of support since everyone is hurting at once.

Even your dearest friends may not be able to give you what you really need. Consider a variety of social contacts including neighbors, co-workers, casual acquaintances, even strangers. Look for people who are good listeners, or those who have suffered a similar loss. Through trial and error you can find out who is helpful and who isn't.

Support comes in many forms: rides, meals, calls, hugs. But don't expect others to guess your needs. You'll have to figure out what you want by listening to your inner voice. When you know what you need and from whom, ask them directly and specifically. "I need company tonight," "a place for Thanksgiving dinner," "someone to come to the cemetery with me."

You might just need a pep talk or some clear advice. Often the best thing a caring friend can offer is simply to listen without judgment. If you mobilize people to help in different ways, you'll have a safety network in place. By carefully identifying your needs, you may discover that valuable support can come from strangers, from films, and from books like this one.

What about getting professional help? When reactions to loss are overwhelming, the support of friends and family may not be enough. Persistent deep depression can prevent healthy grieving. If your grief reaction is so intense and prolonged that sadness sits like a weight on your heart, you may need professional help. If you feel no grief reaction at all, no sorrow or anger or sense of change after suffering a major loss, you may also need advice. Do get professional help if life seems worthless and you feel suicidal. Get help if you have a history of mental illness, have been abusing a substance, or have few sources of support.

A good place to start is with your family doctor. A physician who knows you and your body can evaluate your grief reaction, then offer medication if needed. A prescription can keep you emotionally stable, but guard against over-medicating at the initial stages of loss when you need to be aware of your feelings.

Some doctors aren't trained to do personal counseling or are too busy for it. Other good professional resources include teachers, clergy, funeral directors and psychotherapists. Specialized grief counselors can guide you through the normal grieving process. And remember, it is perfectly all right to shop for a therapist until you find one you truly trust.

You might consider joining a support group that meets regularly. Bound by their common loss, members form a supportive, healing circle. By sharing your concerns and feelings with others, you will grow by giving as well as receiving. There are informal as well as formal support groups dealing with almost every type of loss. Find them in the Yellow Pages, or call a social service agency like the "Y" or United Way.

*I*s there at least one person whom you trust enough to share your sorrow? Or are you locked in silence, thinking no one can possibly understand?

Sometimes we avoid help because we don't want to seem weak or because we're uncomfortable with sympathy. It takes courage to ask for support, courage to allow yourself to be taken care of. Are you brave enough to reach out? You really don't have to bear your losses all alone.

FINDING
FORGIVENESS

Dark thoughts intrude in the gray hours before dawn. Aroused from fitful sleep, the restless mind begins to race. "Why me? Why him? Why now? Why did I deserve this?" Loss brings us face-to-face with our basic vulnerability. Frustration over this helplessness is what makes us feel so angry and so guilty.

Anger is a natural reaction to frustration. Are you in touch with how angry you are over your loss?

🐝 Anger at being deprived, rejected and powerless.

🐝 Anger at doctors and lawyers, at

family and friends, at the one
who left you alone.

🐝 Anger at what might have been.

🐝 Anger at society, fate, God, and
yourself for being imperfect.

🐝 Anger because life just isn't fair.

Take some time to admit your anger
and permit yourself to express it.
Anger suppressed stays unresolved
and is self-destructive. Anger
expressed becomes diffused and
helps you heal. So let your anger bub-
ble up. Write it down, shout it out,
rage at life, practice confrontations
with a friend or with your mirror. Vent
it in the dark and pound your pillow
until your heart feels lighter.

Many people, especially women, are

afraid to express anger, even indirect-
ly. Instead, they automatically turn it
onto themselves and wind up feeling
guilty. Like anger, guilt is a common
reaction to loss. Somehow we feel
responsible when things go wrong, as
if it were our own wrongdoing.

Sometimes guilt can be healthy and
rational—guilt over things that make
good sense. But more often guilt is
unhealthy and irrational—guilt over
senseless things. "I shouldn't have
gone, shouldn't have yelled, shouldn't
have loved so much. I should have
done more, should have given more,
should have loved more." These
impossible "shoulds" can torment you
over and over.

Loss stirs up shame as well as guilt—

the shame of being divorced or unemployed, the shame of having failed. Guilt and shame are forms of anger directed at the self. Because these emotions often increase self-blame, they erode self-esteem. Facing and moving beyond them is an important step in recovery.

How can you reduce your nagging guilt? One way is by giving to others. Volunteering at a social agency, giving to charity, just doing simple good deeds can help you feel less preoccupied with your faults, real or imagined.

Anger is a legitimate emotion—a sign of unresolved conflict and a warning that something needs to be changed. But it's easy to get stuck in anger or guilt and be controlled by them. Are you feeling so angry or so guilty that you can't grieve over your loss?

*H*ealing can't happen if you keep on punishing yourself or the world for things that are beyond anyone's control. Guilt is self-punishment; forgiveness is self-pardon.

Somewhere in your heart there is a well filled with compassion. You may need to draw deeply from that well, but are too afraid to admit your own thirst. You need a loving friend ready to offer you a long drink of tender understanding. You can become that friend by giving to yourself and the world a gift of forgiveness.

EXPECT
TO RECOVER

So many of my patients seem to have no patience. Busy racing around, they lose valuable moments needed for the work of healing. Time is both your greatest asset and biggest challenge on the road to overcoming loss. The hard job isn't saving time, but investing it wisely.

Jenny had no time to prepare for her husband's death. They went out one evening to celebrate their anniversary. By midnight, she found herself beside him in a cardiac care unit and by morning, a widow. Determined not to lean on her grown daughters, she immediately poured herself into managing business affairs and keeping the household going. Jenny was proud of herself for coping, but exhausted by the strain. When friends asked, "How are you doing?" she didn't really know.

It can take months and even years to recover from major loss. You'll need to save your time and strength for conscious grieving, so be careful not to use them up on other things. Simplify your daily routine. Reduce the demands you make on yourself by saying no to others. Jenny decided to stop filling every day with constant tasks. Instead, she began taking some small deliberate steps toward building a new self-image as a widow.

The first steps were very hard: making

that initial phone call for help, going off by herself to a movie. Jenny felt extremely uncomfortable being either alone or with friends. She felt more at ease in "impersonal company," for instance at a library or exercise class. There she could be with people but didn't have to interact with them. By starting slowly and not rushing, she tried to let each phase of the process run its full course to completion.

Healing and recovery are natural processes. Wounds close up and scars fade. The body knows how to mend itself. And so does the mind. Therefore you can expect to eventually heal from your loss. Believing this is half the battle.

You'll probably have cycles of relapse

and rebound, ups and downs in the healing process. But don't misinterpret any of these changes, for the better or for the worse, as permanent. Just keep your expectations in balance, not too high and not too low. Give yourself the luxury of time to convalesce, with no set schedule.

Negative thoughts can be as powerful as positive ones. So it's important to catch yourself when pessimism intrudes. Rehearse happy endings and positive outcomes. Remember that you have a right to live on after loss. By greeting each day with optimism, you are reshaping your future. Try to be patient, because time is truly on your side. Be assured that some day you surely will be able to enjoy life again.

LETTING GO

Six months after his death, Jenny still wore her husband's T-shirts to bed. They held his lingering smell which she wrapped safely around her like a cocoon. Suits hung neatly arranged and waiting in his closet, for time had stopped. Like Sleeping Beauty, she was locked into one phase of her grief, unable to wake up and move on.

You too may be hooked into holding on. For some people, mourning becomes a habit that is just as compelling and satisfying as any addiction. Because Jenny couldn't let go, her grief was turning her loss into a permanent affliction.

Letting go is an active process that has many aspects. Letting go of anger and guilt helps you find forgiveness and inner peace. But letting go also involves objects and routines. Possessions can be deeply poignant. Every year on my birthday, I put on the pearls given me by my friend shortly before she died. This memorial ritual rekindles her memory, bringing her close to me once more.

Deciding what to give and what to keep, what to put away and what to throw away, isn't easy. Facing her husband's belongings forced Jenny to face her denial about the finality of his loss. Are there possessions you need to deal with? Things to clear up or clean out? Things to rearrange or discard? You may have some painful

decisions as you start sorting heir-
looms from junk, sweet mementos
from simple clutter. To grow beyond
loss you must carve out some new
space in your life.

Jenny felt guilty about giving things
away or changing her old routine. She
thought that by keeping everything
intact she proved her loyalty to a long
and loving marriage. However, this
kind of rationalizing is only a way of
postponing the letting go. In the end,
you can't prove love by hanging on to
perpetual sorrow.

Letting go also means giving up
unanswerable questions about why
things turn out the way they do.
Much that happens to us is uncon-
trollable. Once you figure that out,

it's amazing how much freer you feel, freer to let go of trying to control things that can't be controlled.

What makes it so hard to let go after loss? Fear of the unknown often keeps us paralyzed. Loss means an end to things as they were and a realization that life is now fundamentally different. While you are safely anchored in sorrow, you still have a sense of security.

To let go you must cut loose and pull up that anchor. But this is risky business. After all, who knows where the current may carry you, as you float adrift in the sea of tomorrows? And who knows when the next safe harbor will appear on the horizon? This is why the biggest challenge of all is letting go of the fear of letting go. You need to trust yourself and trust life enough to go with the flow.

BODY
COMFORT

The mind, the body, and
the spirit combine to form
the whole self that is you.
Therefore you need to
nurture the body in order
to comfort the self.

When you're feeling downhearted,
try tuning in to the soothing rhythm
heard in the beating of your own
heart. Like a ticking clock, its steady
pulse sends out a vital message that
life goes on after all. When wounded
by loss, the injured self needs tender
loving care. How can you become a
good caregiver? Decide to pamper

yourself. First of all, get enough rest. Rest relieves, restores, refreshes. Yet sleep often eludes those in sorrow. Countless nights of restless insomnia can trigger depression and increase vulnerability.

If you're having trouble sleeping, try some of the following. Gradually reduce your caffeine intake. Exercise moderately late in the day and follow a relaxing bedtime routine at the same time each night to wind down. Don't lie awake for hours obsessing about problems; get up and watch TV in a different room for a while before returning to bed. And be sure to avoid chronic use of sleeping pills.

Remember that rest means more than sleep. Take regular time out during the day to soothe your mind. Find some mindless activity that lets you relax. Schedule breaks for fresh air and sunshine. Perhaps now is the time to use up personal leave or vacation days. Anticipating a long weekend ahead for rest and recovery can lift your spirits.

To nurture your body you have to nourish it. But appetites often shift after loss. Some people use food for emotional comfort and eat constantly, while others find food offensive and eat haphazardly. In either case, you need to schedule three solid meals a day, even if you're not hungry. This lets your body know that you respect and won't neglect it. Nourishment is essential for healing, so this is not a good time for crash dieting. Remember that the best way to control junk food bingeing is by eating regular meals.

Of course, food is not for the flesh alone. Chocolate can soothe the injured soul. Be sure to enjoy some treat food each day to nourish your hungry heart. But beware of addictive or compulsive habits—things that taste or feel so good you can't control them. Addictions are often used as self-medication to ease the pain of loss. Too much alcohol, coffee, candy, or even exercise can be a warning signal for help.

Your body also craves the comfort of human contact. Hugging and holding are natural tools for healing. All good nurses practice the hands-on power of personal touch. So start reaching out for more touching in your life. Hold hands with friends, cuddle kids and pets, get a massage or back rub.

When chimps want the comfort of contact, they groom each other. In fact, grooming is a great way to enjoy touch from yourself as well as from others. Go ahead and invest in some personal grooming. Pamper your hair or skin. Get a manicure, pedicure, or other beauty cure that enhances body image. Part of the beauty of looking good is how good it can make you feel.

Movement is another basic body need. In one survey, mourners rated exercise as the very best medicine of all for healing. No, you don't have to sweat out in a gym. Just begin by walking a few minutes a day. Then gradually increase the goal as you discover the joy of moving through space. Try putting on some gentle music. Swing and sway as you make beautiful motions alone or with another.

Music is a universal source of energy and pleasure. You can never overdose on it, so go ahead and freely indulge all your passions. Listen to music regularly, sing out in the car and hum in the shower. Babies are naturally soothed by lullabies, and also by being rocked or rubbed. Many such "childish" pleasures can reduce stress and ease pain—for instance, simple sensual comforts like sucking sweets, smelling flowers, or floating in water. Why not indulge your body in some of these gentle pastimes?

Minding the body really matters. By listening to what your body needs, you'll hear the healing rhythms of the physical self. The sound of recovery has a special beat. If you tune in to your body's messages you can pick up the beat of life and learn a basic step in the dance of recovery.

SPIRITUAL COMFORT

Loss has been described as a spiritual wound, mourning as the art of spiritual healing. Rabbi Harold Kushner wrote *When Bad Things Happen to Good People* after the difficult death of his young son. In the book, he concludes that faith can transcend tragedy. "In the end, we stop asking why something has happened . . . but start asking how we will respond. What we intend to do now that it has happened."

Human beings have a conscience and a sense of free will. We question our place in the grand design of things. We want to believe that birth and death and love are more than mere random acts. Faith often forms the basis of belief as we seek some greater sense of purpose in life.

However, when loss hits hard its impact can undermine your faith in a meaningful world. You're faced with a spiritual crisis. If, in fact, some master plan has set things in motion, why is senseless tragedy built into that plan? Those who believe in a supreme being sometimes have an even harder time than nonbelievers. Feeling betrayed by their faith, they ask, "Why weren't my prayers heard? Why did God abandon me?" Loss of faith then becomes a source of pain added on top of the primary loss.

Perhaps your own sense of faith comes and goes, along with waves of

sorrow. Perhaps you've found yourself
supremely angry at the Supreme
Being. Remember that forgiveness is
part of the healing process.

> *B*y forgiving God you
> start to forgive yourself and
> to accept a world that
> remains imperfect.

Loss challenges us to find new ways of
communing with the holiness within
and around us. Spiritual dialogue can
take many forms. Some find solace in
traditional religious prayers, while others must create their own personal
style. Prayer can help us end feelings
of isolation, and tap into hidden
reserves of faith and courage that are
otherwise inaccessible.

Have you contacted a religious leader for spiritual support? They have the training to help you find a pathway to renewed faith. They can recommend books, prayer groups, or retreats. Don't think you have to belong to a specific congregation to ask for help. One of the primary functions of all religious groups is to provide comfort to those in need.

Many holy books such as the Bible are filled with tragic tales of brothers who kill and mates who deceive, of floods and plagues and suffering. One message to be found in these accounts is that loss is a universal part of life. They imply that to be fully human is to have a range of profound experiences, from the tragic to the sublime.

*A*lthough grief may
shake your faith, new faith
often grows from grief.
A deeper and more mature
understanding of the
divine dimension of life
can emerge from your
struggle with loss.

As Kushner writes, "I think of my son
and all that his life taught me, and I
realize how much I have lost and how
much I have gained. Yesterday seems
less painful, and I am not afraid of
tomorrow."

REMEMBERING

Hard as you may try, you can't stop time. It moves on relentlessly, leaving behind only memories of life's loves and life's losses. These unique memory traces drawn by the passage of time have been called the imagery of the inner world. We freeze-frame special images and carefully preserve them in the cool corners of the mind. While memories are powerful tools in the healing process, they must be handled with care. Memories can be hurtful as well as helpful, destructive as well as constructive.

After being injured in an accident, Kevin spent months trying to regain the use of his legs. As he struggled with immobility, he described how hard it was to see photos of himself a few years earlier playing tennis for his college team. Kevin hated to be reminded of all he had been and all he had lost.

Memories create longing. Like Kevin, we want our health back, our job back, our mate back. We prefer real tennis and real love to the mere memory of it, for even the best memory can't substitute for the real thing. And of course, not all memories are good ones. Haunting images intrude like nightmares, reawakening trauma that is best laid to rest.

Yet memories of what you were or what you had before your loss are an essential part of who you are today. To remember and to reflect on your memories is like reuniting with an old friend or with a forgotten dream.

> *O*ne sure sign of recovery is
> the ability to reclaim and
> relive the past without being
> overcome by it.

Months after his injury, Kevin had part-
ly recovered. He could now watch
videos of his championship tennis
matches with composure and even
pleasure. He had begun to incorporate
his past with a new sense of future
possibilities.

If some memories feel too painful for
you right now, be patient. The healing
process will allow you to gradually
own them again and restore to you the
comforting gift of remembrance.

Communities build memorials and conduct ceremonies to honor the lost and to sustain the living. At the Viet Nam veterans' memorial in Washington, DC, the names of the dead are carved in marble. Visitors often reach out to touch the surface of the stone as if it were alive. And in this hands-on gesture they get in touch with emotions buried deep inside.

Memorial rituals can help us reach within to tap a tender source of memory and reclaim valuable feelings that have been lost. You too may find it comforting to create a personal memorial to honor your loss: a scrapbook with letters, a small altar in the home with pictures or souvenirs, a rose garden dedicated to a special memory.

Have you thought about creating your own ritual of remembrance? This could be a preplanned event which is dedicated to grieving and healing. Such rituals can be used to mark a shift in the way you mourn or as an official end to mourning. Some people use a formal ritual such as a religious service. Others create a personal rite to mark the memory of a loss.

Pick a day with meaning—a birthday or anniversary. Go to a special place, read something aloud or listen to a favorite song. It might be a solemn rite, but it could also be a warm celebration of what once was and is no more. Whether you plan this ritual alone or with others, it can nurture you with the healing power of remembrance.

EXPRESSING
FEELINGS

Psychotherapy has been called "the talking cure." Yet good therapists may say very little. They encourage *you* to do the talking while *they* do the listening. In therapy as in life, monologue can prove as useful as dialogue. Remember Hamlet's soliloquy. After suffering outrageous misfortune, Hamlet wonders aloud whether life after loss is worth living—whether he wants "to be or not to be?" And as he ponders this question aloud, answers drift up from the deepest chambers of his heart.

*W*hy not start a therapeutic dialogue with yourself and break the taboo of talking about feelings?

Find the thoughts, form the words, speak and hear them. Allow your mind to wander spontaneously where it will. No censoring. No criticism. No judgment. Forget about grammar and style. Just let your feelings flow onto paper, onto tape, onto the evening air. Don't worry about how to say it right. Just say it in some way.

When her mother died, Elena experienced an overwhelming sense of emptiness. "I thought my heart would burst. I kept wanting to talk to her, to explain, to ask, to remember. Suddenly I realized that I missed my past, and I began writing a letter to my children." She tried to describe her mother's life and family history. Recalling details was difficult at first, but she found that memories came to her during sleep. The more she wrote, the easier it became. "It was as if I had been handed a ball of string. I took one end and pulled. The string kept coming and coming."

A bereavement counselor recommends writing a series of letters and reading them aloud in front of a photograph of the deceased. In the first letter you try to express thanks for specific things the loved one did for you. In the second you express regrets and apologize for things you did that may have hurt him or her. You might also try a third one written to yourself as if the deceased were answering your first two notes. By writing such letters you have a chance to say things that were left unsaid and to find closure in the relationship.

One study found that people who started keeping journals had stronger immune systems and less illness than before they began writing. Journals don't have to be kept regularly. Just write whenever a thought wells up. Keeping a diary or letters written over time can give you a reassuring record of your own recovery process.

Of course, it's hard to put sorrow into words. Everyday language seems inadequate to describe a profound loss. Perhaps you are better with images than with words. What would an image of your pain look like? Get a blank page and just start to scribble or doodle, even if you aren't very artistic. Or get some clay and feel the shape and texture of grief by kneading and smoothing its contours. Artistic expression of all kinds can open up feelings, regardless of your level of talent.

FROM STRESS TO PEACE

Many of us chronically check our time pieces in the race to make peace with time. Up against the clock, we hurriedly piece together the measured moments of our lives. Pressures, schedules, deadlines—all pull in different directions at once. Stress builds whenever there's too much to do and too little time to do it.

> *E*very loss and every change sends stressful waves of instability. And of course, major loss causes major stress.

Bob was laid off many months ago. He feels that time is running out as his savings dwindle and he describes a growing sense of inner tension. "I wake up anxious and irritable, like I'm wired so tight I can explode at the drop of a hat. I guess that's why my kids have learned to keep their distance," he observes.

Stress leads to distress, and eventually to burnout, breakdowns, and breakups. After months of unemployment, Bob's wife is doing a lot of crying, his son is doing a lot of fighting, and his own chronic back pain has gotten much worse. Stress weakens the body's natural defense systems, leaving us more vulnerable to illness and injury.

As you rebound from loss, remember that you're already fragile, so be gentle with yourself. Try to recognize the sources of your stress and reduce them whenever you can. For instance, postpone major decision-making until the acute phase of your grief reaction is over. Don't take on greater responsibilities right now, and try to avoid situations that are sure to cause conflict. Perhaps one of the most useful things you can do is to get a book on stress reduction and devote time to it each day.

Bob did some reading and discovered that, for him, solitude was a healing antidote to stress. He also found a safe haven in his own car. Parked on a scenic overlook he could claim a peaceful retreat from the pressures of the day. There, he could simply "be in the here and now," with no phones, no faxes, no interruptions. And no need to explain himself or sell himself. Time felt kinder in the comfort of silence where he could slow down the ticking of his inner clock.

Has your own loss left you so overworked and overbooked that you overlook your need to be alone? Why not escape from stress to a quiet island of repose. Explore a solitary path on the road to recovery, a detour for meditation, reflection, and introspection. When conversation with others becomes tiring, let them know you appreciate their concern but you really need some private time out. Tucked safely in the serenity of solitude your stress may subside, and you can start to hear those secrets that your soul reveals.

LAUGHTER
NATURE, AND
CREATIVITY

Should we laugh in the face of loss?
Comedian Joan Rivers thinks so.
Using her professional failures and
the tragedy of her husband's suicide
as background, she's been teaching
mourners how to smile through their
tears. First she asks audiences filled
with bereaved people to turn to
someone next to them and dutifully
recite out loud: "I'm so very glad
that . . ." After a long pause, she
finally gives them the rest of the sen-
tence to complete . . . *"I'm not you!"*
and they burst out laughing.

Joan tells them they are each entitled to a "weekend of wallowing." For two whole days they should list every terrible thing that has ever happened to them, and feel very sorry for themselves. But on Monday they must start a new list of all the positive things in their life.

Is it proper to joke about a husband's suicide, as she does? Isn't there shame when smiles dissolve your sorrow? Isn't there guilt when joy disrupts your mourning? Play has been called the flip side of grief. As Joan Rivers plays with words, she teases and tickles her audience out of their gloom. She treats life as a stage that must be filled with as much comedy as tragedy.

Even though you're hurting, don't be afraid to become a player on this new stage of your life. Let your lighter side emerge through the joy of a good joke. At first you may feel like you're just going through the motions. Of course, the outside can look happy while the inside is still aching.

> *Y*et the body can also fool itself. As you hear yourself laughing and feeling your face smiling, your mood will actually shift.

In fact, laughter may even help you heal from serious illness. It seems that watching comedy and reading humor speeds up recovery. And nature is also helpful. Some hospitals have harnessed the healing power of nature by building restful garden rooms. Patients report feeling renewed after spending time surrounded by plants, and depressed patients perk up when a fish bowl is put beside them.

So be sure to take a brief detour into nature as you journey back onto the main stage of life. Spend time watching birds chasing overhead, or clouds casting shadows. Let the breeze play with your hair and the sunset spill into your eyes. Drink in this glorious world and nourish yourself with the splendor of creation.

Artists sometimes find a link between loss and creativity. In the fertile soil of their grief they discover new seeds germinating. Why not search within your sorrow for the creative energy buried there? To compensate for things which are no more, try creating things which never were before.

- 🐝 **Learn something**—poems, jokes, card tricks; then teach them to a child.

- 🐝 **Collect something**—shells, driftwood; then show them to a child.

- 🐝 **Write something**—poetry, letters; then read them to a child.

- 🐝 **Make something**—pies, pictures; then share them with a child.

Such simple creative acts can enrich the world as well as the self. Using humor and nature and creativity, you can cultivate new meaning after loss.

GROWING
BEYOND LOSS

After twenty-something years of marriage, Laura's husband left her for a much younger replacement. Feeling stunned, she struggled through a nasty divorce. Besides losing his love, Laura also lost their shared life together and their shared future.

Unfortunately, she was left with something called a "spoiled identity." For twenty years she had believed she was happily married, but now that view of her past was spoiled. For twenty years she had expected to grow old as a couple, and now that view of her future was spoiled. While Laura can reclaim parts of her self-esteem that remain intact, she can't restore her former image. Like it or not, a core of that old identity is lost. She must reconstruct a new unspoiled one.

Fortunately, Laura has been left with something else: a chance to grow. "Don't worry, I'm sure I'll survive," she says bravely. But growing and thriving are more than just surviving.

> *T*o grow beyond loss you must first let go, then move ahead by trying on new roles and traveling on new roads.

In a sense, each loss is a pregnant pause in the process of personal growth. Just as time provides a resource, loss also presents a window of opportunity. It may not be easy for Laura to clear off that window and peer through the haze of uncertainty into the future. Her ultimate challenge is to pass courageously through the familiar framework and into the unknown. In this way, her loss can become a passage forward into life. In this way she can discover a path to recovery.

Now is the time for Laura to seek newness. Perhaps the time is also ripe for you to do the same. After a loss, growth and change are needed for healing to progress. Take time to explore new people, places, and possibilities. Make time to re-do your image: re-style your hair and refresh your clothes. Time to remodel your space: remove the drapes and rearrange the rooms. Time to pursue interests: recover old talents and uncover new ones. Time to explore exotic foods and novel experiences. Life takes on new meaning as you look for new meaning in life.

After denial, anger, and active grieving are behind you, change is the challenge ahead. Through change you can restore your vitality with the thrill of doing something wonderful for the very first time. Through change a new intact identity will gradually emerge. You may find it is stronger, wiser, and perhaps even nicer than the one you reluctantly left behind.

RECOGNIZE RECOVERY

Healing isn't always obvious. Subtle changes take place gradually, for it's a process, not an outcome. This is why you might overlook your own recovery, even when it's happening right before your eyes.

The road to recovery isn't smooth but fraught with bumpy ups and downs, with puddles and potholes. So it's useful to take stock of how far you've come on your healing journey.

What should you look for as signs of progress? Slowly but surely you're sleeping better, thinking clearer, crying less and smiling more. You've gained greater control of your emotions and aren't so easily overwhelmed by them. You're less obsessed with your loss and can talk about it more easily. You feel freer to choose when and how to grieve. You seem less preoccupied with yourself, and more patient with everyone, including yourself.

The waves of pain don't come as often and they don't knock you over as easily. You're thinking less about the past, looking forward as well as backward, reaching out toward the future less fearfully. Sometimes you realize that hours or even days have passed when you're nearly free of pain. You feel a renewed interest in giving love and receiving it.

It may be helpful to identify some of the things you can now do that were impossible at first. Your list might include (1) accepting invitations, (2) staying comfortably home alone, (3) asking for help, etc. Don't expect all of these things to be happening at once or at the same rate. Do look for small signs of progress.

Savor the sight of your own smiling face in the mirror. Catch yourself buying plants or making plans and recognize how much better you're feeling. Why not celebrate by splurging on a gift or throwing a coming-out party in recognition of recovery? As you drink in the happiness of healing, remember to give a toast of thanks to those who helped you along the way.

ACCEPTANCE

I miss my friend a lot, especially on my birthday or whenever I need her pearls of wisdom to help me cope. Yet I also know how much better off I am to have loved and lost her, than to have lived without her love in my life. Her death has taught me something about valuing what I do have, and accepting what I can't have.

Acceptance is essential in overcoming loss. It isn't a final stage or goal, however, but a continuous process. We need to:

- ☙ accept reality and overcome denial.
- ☙ accept sorrow and actively grieve.
- ☙ accept anger and express it.
- ☙ accept guilt and forgive.

- ☞ accept help and seek support.
- ☞ accept the past and embrace its memories.
- ☞ accept what is final and let go.
- ☞ accept recovery and welcome new growth.
- ☞ accept that loss occurs and we can't control it.
- ☞ accept that bad things *do* happen to good people.

Acceptance doesn't mean angry resignation: "I'll have to make do, but I'll hate every minute." Acceptance doesn't mean passive resignation: "I'll have to make do, since I can't do anything about it." Acceptance does mean actively reaching out toward loss and stretching your personal space to embrace it.

In this way acceptance helps you convert loss into something that leads to growth. Once you have truly absorbed a loss as your own, you can honor it as a turning point in your development. Acceptance leads to wholeness and a sense of integrity, which helps restore inner peace.

Remember, you weren't singled out for pain and you aren't in it alone. Just look around. The world is full of grieving people, all struggling to overcome their own losses, just as you are. Loss digs a well that can later fill up with joy. And the deeper the well, the greater may be your capacity for experiencing life.

An act of love sets each life going. Wound up like a big gold watch, we